Original title:
The Poetry of Propagation

Copyright © 2025 Creative Arts Management OÜ
All rights reserved.

Author: Kieran Blackwood
ISBN HARDBACK: 978-1-80581-789-5
ISBN PAPERBACK: 978-1-80581-316-3
ISBN EBOOK: 978-1-80581-789-5

Emergence of Enchantment

In a garden where gnomes play,
Seeds chuckle in silly ballet,
A sprout pops its head, takes a bow,
"I'm the star of the show, look at me now!"

With worms wearing hats made of leaves,
And ants telling tales of old heaves,
The daisies dance in twirling delight,
As the sun gives its wink to the night.

Bees argue over the best flower,
While roses boast of their sweet power,
The daisies just giggle with glee,
"Who knew gardening could be this free?"

So come join the fun with your spade,
Where silliness blooms and no plans are laid,
A world where laughter grows oh so tall,
In gardens of magic where we can all haul!

Stirring the Soil

With a shovel, I dance, twirl, and spin,
Waving my arms, letting the fun begin,
"Hey, Mr. Mole, get out of my way!
I'm turning the earth where my veggies will play!"

Earthworms deliver their best stand-up,
"Why did the carrot refuse the cup?
Because it was too radish for tea!" they all snort,
As I till and chuckle in my grassy court.

Compost piles gossiping low,
"Did you hear the rumor? Lettuce is a show!"
Tomatoes blush, all shade and flair,
"Let's just say, we ripen with care!"

So grab your gloves, join in the fight,
Come feel the giggles, oh what a sight,
With garden tricks and laughter in tow,
In the soil, our joy starts to grow!

A Symphony of Soil

In the ground a secret hum,
Worms wiggle to the beat's thrum.
Roots tap dance without a care,
Overhead, the breeze joins the flair.

Seeds in pockets, a jolly crew,
Sprouting dreams in shades of blue.
Sun and rain, a crazy mix,
Nature's band plays its tricks.

Cradle of Creations

Dandelions blow with a sneeze,
Tickling noses like summer tease.
In every petal, a story's spun,
Bees buzz laughter, oh what fun!

Puddle splashes, mud pie delight,
Children dance in total flight.
Each giggle echoes, nature's cheer,
Life's a party when spring is near!

Nature's Narrative

Leafy tales whisper, 'Look at me!'
Branches wave like wild and free.
Squirrels chatter in chaotic tone,
Sharing gossip they've all known.

Roses blush, it's all a show,
Thorns bring giggles, oh what woe!
Petals drop like little jokes,
Nature's laughter, full of pokes.

Flora's Footprints

Tiny sprouts with giant dreams,
Dance among the sunlight beams.
Each bloom a smile, a sunny face,
Flowers frolic, a wild race.

Vines canoodle in a twist,
Climbing high, they can't resist.
Garden jokes play hide and seek,
While roots giggle, oh so sleek!

Stanzas of the Sun

Bright sun wore shades, oh so cool,
A radiant star, playing the fool.
It glimmers and jokes, in skies so wide,
Chasing the clouds, like a cheeky guide.

Lizards sunbathe, lounging about,
While flowers giggle, without a doubt.
They whisper secrets, in golden rays,
While bees join in, to dance and praise.

Rhythm of Roots

Roots tap dance beneath the ground,
Grooving and moving, without a sound.
They share their tales with all the worms,
Who wiggle in time to the earthy terms.

Aquirreling squirrel joins the beat,
With nuts in hand, it can't be beat.
The tiny seeds hum songs of mirth,
As they deepen in soil, for all they're worth.

Blossoming Thoughts

Thoughts bloom like daisies, wild and bright,
Each one a giggle, a burst of light.
They twirl and swirl in the soft spring air,
Crafting wild dreams, without a care.

Poppies pop up, declaring delight,
While tulips gossip under moonlight.
They're crafting tales of romantic spree,
With laughter that sways, oh can't you see?

The Dance of the Dandelion

Dandelions waltz, in the breeze they fly,
With puffs of fluff dancing up to the sky.
They giggle and wiggle, in fields so green,
Their joy so contagious, it's rarely seen.

A child makes a wish, as they blow them away,
Dreams in the air, where the wishes play.
These merry little sprites, so carefree and bold,
In the dance of the dandelions, stories unfold.

Weaving Wilderness

In the forest, roots take a leap,
Squirrels plot while the saplings peep.
They giggle as they stretch and twine,
Nature's dance is quite divine.

Vines tie a knot, a cheeky embrace,
While fungi wear their funny face.
The trees play hide and seek in style,
With a rustling laugh and a leafy smile.

One with the Flora

The daisies gossip in a row,
While bumblebees spin tales of woe.
"Why did the tulip cross the street?"
"To show the rose, it can't be beat!"

Cacti cracking jokes in the sun,
While fickle ferns just want some fun.
With giggles from the blooms all around,
Who knew plants could be so profound?

Blossoms of Belonging

A sunflower shouts, "I'm the best!"
While lilacs argue with zest.
"Petunias! You're just a rainbow mishap,"
They roll on rhizomes, a floral clap.

In the pot, they're all a bit nutty,
Sharing soil makes us so buddy.
With a wink and a sway of their heads,
These blossoms know how to spread the threads.

Flickers of Fertility

Seeds are chuckling as they take flight,
"Catch me if you can!" they say with delight.
In the breeze, they twirl and swirl,
Nature's little seeds doing a whirl.

Little pods popping, what a scene!
Creating chaos, fulfilling the dream.
With laughter planted in every sprout,
In this garden, there's no room for doubt.

Transience of Petals

Petals dance in skirts so bright,
Flirting with bees in daylight.
But when the wind gives a hearty shove,
They tumble down, not in love!

Where do they go when they take flight?
A vaudeville show, a whimsical sight.
They land on dogs, in stew or pie,
So many places for petals to lie!

Tides of Transformation

The tide rolls in, with a slap and a splash,
Crabs scuttle sideways, in a zany dash.
Seasalt jokes are all they share,
While starfish giggle without a care.

Seashells whisper of mermaids' schemes,
In the surf, they'll plot as it gleams.
Each wave a punchline, surfboards in tow,
Surf's up for laughter, let the humor flow!

Harbingers of Change

In the garden, gnomes take bets,
On which plant's next for funny sets.
One flops over, wearing a frown,
While carrots sprout in a sleepy town.

Rabbits host meetings, munching on greens,
Crafting the quirkiest of routines.
With every nibble, new tales arise,
So who knew veggies could be so wise?

Cadence of the Canopy

Under branches where squirrels tease,
They chatter jokes among the leaves.
A bird drops a note, oh what a scene,
Turns out it's just a leafy cuisine!

Roots wiggle down, holding steady in jest,
Claiming the title of earth's best guest.
Clouds look down, they're giggling too,
It's a canopy party, just for you!

Blossoms of Resilience

In the garden where blooms explode,
A daisy dodges a pesky toad.
It chuckles at weeds, with roots so wide,
Who knew in mud, such laughs could hide?

Petunias gossip with vibrant flair,
While violets play truth or dare.
With a wink from the sun, they start to tease,
What's more fun than a flower's breeze?

Notes from Nature's Choir

A squirrel strums on an acorn drum,
While bees buzz by, just having fun.
The trees clap hands in the gentle wind,
Nature's giggles have no end!

The crickets croon with rhythmic delight,
As fireflies twinkle, shining bright.
A chorus of frogs joins in the glee,
All in tune, wild and free!

Threads of Life Interwoven

In the web of life, we spin and twirl,
A caterpillar slips, oh what a whirl!
Flower threads fly like colorful confetti,
Sewing joy, it's always ready!

Butterflies dance in the sunlight glow,
While worms wiggle on the ground below.
Each thread connects in a quirky thread,
With laughter blooming, no need for dread!

Rebirth in Every Petal

Buds pop open, a surprise to see,
A shy flower peeks out, giggling with glee!
In the pollen party, all join the dance,
Each petal a laugh, giving life a chance.

When raindrops fall, they play on the ground,
And grass blades nod, joyfully unbound.
Every bloom laughs, a perfect sweet jest,
In the wild world, we're all guests!

Lyrical Landscapes

In a garden where the daisies dance,
A rabbit winks, takes a chance.
He juggles carrots with great might,
While worms cheer from both left and right.

Tulips giggle, tickling the breeze,
As ants form a band beneath the trees.
Singing tunes of sugary glee,
While bees hum along, in sweet harmony.

Clouds drift by with a playful pout,
A sunbeam shouts, 'Let's twist and shout!'
Like the flowers who sway in a tune,
Each petal a dancer under the moon.

Rain drops chuckle, a soft little splash,
Each puddle reflects a splashy stash.
A duck quacks jokes to the fish below,
A comedy act in nature's show!

Sprouts of Serenity

In pots of clay, a cactus dreams,
It wishes for water, or so it seems.
But the flowers mock with petals bright,
   Sipping the dew 'til late in the night.

A sunflower leans like it's got a crush,
On the wobbly bee—oh, what a rush!
They tango sweetly, oh what a sight,
   In a whirl of yellow, oh pure delight.

The roots gossip deep beneath the ground,
"Who wore it best?" is the talk all around.
With pantry debates on the freshest greens,
They laugh at the weeds and their silly schemes.

Even the stones have a tale or two,
About old moss and the morning dew.
Each sprout has dreams that are wild and strange,
In this giggle-filled garden where nothing's mundane!

Cadence of the Cosmos

Stars playful twinkle in cosmic attire,
While comets dash by like a cosmic choir.
A moon chuckles softly, 'Look at me spin!'
As planets roll laughter in a galactic din.

Jupiter jigs, Saturn spins rings,
While asteroids clash like they're kings with their flings.
In cosmic concerts, they play tag at dawn,
With a tickle from light and a wink from the dawn.

Black holes laugh, 'What's inside, we don't say!'
As they gobble up stardust without any pay.
Galaxies swirl in a polka dot groove,
In the ballroom of space, they effortlessly move.

A meteor shower tosses sparkly jokes,
As the universe fills with giggles and pokes.
Each twinkling star, a mischievous sprite,
Dancing through dark, what a celestial sight!

Colorful Currents

In a stream where the fish wear tiny hats,
They gossip about boats and all of that.
A frog croaks, 'Hey, I can tap dance too!'
And the lilies all giggle, like they always do.

The turtles, they sunbathe, all in a line,
Discussing who'd win in a race, oh so fine.
With each splashy bet, they laugh till they snort,
In this rippling humor, all fish want to court.

A snail takes his time, declares, 'I'll float!',
In a leaf that sets sail, what a quirky boat!
While the otters glide past, giggling so loud,
As the river winks back, so smooth and proud.

With breezes that play tug-of-war with trees,
And whispers of secrets carried with ease,
In this colorful current where laughter flows,
Every drop holds a joke that nobody knows!

Harvesting Hope

In the garden of dreams we sow,
We plant our seeds, oh, watch them grow!
With wobbly feet, a sprout does dance,
While squirrels plot their nutty chance.

Watering cans spill like laughter's sound,
Blooming wisdom spreads all around.
The weeds whisper jokes beneath the light,
As sunbeams tickle the leaves in flight.

Luminescence in Bloom

Petals drenched in morning dew,
They giggle brightly in a colorful hue.
Bees don tiny hats, so dapper and nice,
They cha-cha 'round like they own the spice!

Lights dance in the twilight's embrace,
With flowers making a comic face.
A tulip jokes, 'I'm the best in class!'
While daisies laugh till they nearly crass.

Charting the Seasons

Spring's just a toddler with grass-stained knees,
Summer's a party with ice cream, please!
Autumn's a joker, tossing leaves with glee,
While Winter plays games of hide-and-freeze.

Calendars flip, giggles fly,
Each season's a pie, oh my, oh my!
Nature's handwriting in the sky,
You never know who's passing by!

Fragments of Flora

Hitchhiking bees on a wandering vine,
Lyrics of flowers in a quirky line.
Pansies wear pajamas, so comfy and bright,
While sunflowers debate who has the best height.

Petals swirl like confetti thrown,
Whimsical whispers in gardens grown.
Nature's comic strip, a vibrant scene,
With giggles of green in a marigold sheen.

Resounding Bloom

In gardens where odd seeds are tossed,
They sprout with laughter, no matter the cost.
A flower that sings, what a curious sight,
Dancing in breezes, oh, what pure delight!

With petals of polka dots, bright and loud,
They party for bees, inviting the crowd.
Whispers of colors make insects buzz,
What's all this fuss? Just nature's buzz!

Snapdragons chime with a jolly good cheer,
They snap and they crackle, as if to say, "Here!"
A pitch-perfect bloom that croons in the day,
Making the garden a hip cabaret!

So let's plant some giggles, let joy take its flight,
In fields of wild humor, from morning till night.
With roots that are joking and vines that all rhyme,
This flora of laughter is truly sublime!

Ciphers in the Canopy

Beneath the leaves, secrets float and glide,
Whispers of squirrels, the mischief they hide.
A riddle of branches, tangled and sweet,
Where giggles of sunlight and shadow compete.

The trees wear their laughter like jackets of green,
With owls telling jokes, what a curious scene!
With riddles in bark and humor in the air,
Nature's own stand-up, beyond compare!

Acorns drop down with a plop and a thud,
"Hey, watch out below!" as they land with a thud.
Leaves rustle and chuckle at the squirrel's clumsiness,
It's all just a game, this leafy funniness!

And as the sun sets, the whispers ignite,
In a canopy dance, a spectacular sight.
With twirls and a spin, they prance in the dark,
Those ciphers in branches leave an everlasting mark.

Verses of the Vines

With twirling green tendrils that twist and that twine,
They've written their letters, in nature's own line.
Grapes giggle softly, on vines they do climb,
Composing their ballads, all in good time.

Oh, what a frolic, as the shoots make their way,
Tangled in laughter, they sway and they play.
"Let's see who can reach the top by nightfall!"
The vines are a chorus, they sing and they sprawl!

One vine shimmies, while another does 'boogie',
In this verdant dance-off, there's never a droogie!
Each grape with a wink, each leaf with a jest,
In this leafy karaoke, they're all at their best!

As morning dew sparkles on their cheeky parade,
They wrap up their sonnets, in laughter they wade.
With verses composed in the good of the sun,
These vines, they're a jest, but oh, what fun!

Vibrations of Vitality

The meadow hums with a bouncy refrain,
Where daisies and dandelions dance in the rain.
They wiggle and jiggle, like kids on a spree,
Shouting "We're here, come join us for tea!"

Crickets strum strings on a skateboard of grass,
With rhythms of life, as the minutes all pass.
"Hey, listen to us, we're the band of the spot!"
It's a concert of chuckles, it's getting quite hot!

Butterflies twirl with a flair of the bold,
Swapping their stories, both funny and old.
From blossoms to beetles, the fun never fades,
In this vibrant bazaar of life's grand parades!

As dusk paints the sky with hues of delight,
They giggle in shadows, the laughter takes flight.
With a sprinkle of glee and a dash of sweet cheer,
The vibrations of life keep the laughter near!

Petal Poetry

In gardens where daisies dance and tease,
Bees craft their rhymes beneath the trees.
Sunflowers giggle with seeds spread wide,
The tulips whisper of love, side by side.

As the wind carries jokes through the air,
Lilies laugh loud, without a care.
Each blossom joins in a colorful play,
Nature's verses brighten the day.

Illuminated Endeavors

A bright little bud with dreams in the sun,
Wonders if growing is actually fun.
With roots in the dirt and leaves in the sky,
It cracks silly jokes as the butterflies fly.

In this quest for growth, they stumble and twirl,
Petals poke humor at the world's great whirl.
A rose with a pun, oh what a sight!
In the green world, laughter takes flight.

The Blooming Tapestry

A tapestry woven with laughter and sprout,
Where each silly seed has a story to tout.
Geraniums grin with their vibrant display,
While marigolds chuckle at clouds in dismay.

Chrysanthemums giggle, their petals a tease,
Sharing sweet secrets with buzzing expertise.
Together they bloom, a fantastical crew,
In the garden of whimsy, just waiting for dew.

Nectar of Narratives

Bee tales of honey that tickle the ears,
Fluttering stories that bring lots of cheers.
With petals to write them, they dance in delight,
Each drop of nectar a story ignites.

Forget all your worries, come join in the fun,
With blossoms that giggle as bright as the sun.
In this world of bloom, creativity flows,
Nature's own theater, where laughter bestows.

Wisps of Wonder

A seed once dreamed of a grand ballet,
But tripped on roots, oh how they sway!
The sun giggled, giving a wink,
As flowers danced, no time to think.

A breeze came by with a cheeky laugh,
Tickling leaves on their leafy path.
A butterfly joined in on the fun,
Saying, "Why walk when we can run?"

The petals pranced, a colorful sight,
While worms recited silly poetry at night.
Together they twirled, oh what a scene,
In a garden where nothing's too serene!

With each little sprout came a giggly cheer,
As critters gathered, drawing near.
In this joyful chaos, life unfurled,
A comic ballet of the plant world!

Cultivating Connections

In the soil, friendships take root,
A turnip met a dancing beetroot.
They twirled in circles, all muddy and bold,
Telling tales of days of old.

A snail slipped by with dreams so grand,
Sharing secrets of the garden band.
He said, "Life's a party, don't be shy,
Join the rhythm, just give it a try!"

The daisies laughed, with petals in curls,
Swaying like kids on merry-go-worlds.
Blushing tomatoes, they joined the jam,
Spelling friendship with a great big spam.

As the sun dipped low, they gathered in close,
For a night of chatter, they'd all engross.
In every sprout, there was ember and fire,
Cultivating joy, oh, how they inspire!

Tender Tendrils

Little tendrils stretching for the sky,
Chasing after clouds as they float by.
"What if we link?" one vine did giggle,
"And share our laughs while doing a wiggle?"

A cucumber chimed in, all green and grand,
"I'll bring the snacks, let's make a stand!"
Then they all quipped, in a viney embrace,
"Let's start a joke-off, a giggly race!"

With every twist and turn, they marveled,
At all the silly plans they'd garbled.
The pumpkins chuckled, each round and wide,
"Why be serious? We can't hide!"

So in the garden, amid joy and glee,
Tender tendrils danced, wild and free.
With laughter and fun, they all intertwined,
In a leafy playground of the silliest kind!

Kinetic Kinetics

In a world where sprouts move and sway,
Dancing to tunes of a sunny ballet.
The sunflowers spun with a gleeful twirl,
While the cabbages giggled, giving a whirl.

Each bud had rhythm, each leaf a beat,
Doing the tango with wiggly feet.
"I'm the sap-ologist," said one sprout with flair,
"Here to shake things up and spread the air!"

A wild carrot jumped, giving a cheer,
With a coconut laying nearby, oh dear!
They rolled and they tumbled, all joyous and free,
In this kinetic festivity, can't you see?

So if you ever feel a little shy,
Join the garden dance with a hop and a cry.
For in every movement, there's laughter anew,
Kinetic kinetics just waiting for you!

The Narrative of Nurturing

In a garden, seeds do dance,
They plot their growth, a grand romance.
With water sprinkles, they take a chance,
Making veggies seem so smart in their stance.

A carrot debates with a haughty pea,
"I'm closer to the ground, can't you see?"
The pea just laughs, full of glee,
"But in pots, my friends all envy me!"

To dandelions, we tip our hats,
They pop up everywhere, like pesky chats.
While daisies giggle, like clumsy acrobats,
In this odd world, all nature chats.

Roots tangle tightly, a wild affair,
Whispering secrets of who goes where.
With leaves as hats, they're debonair,
In this green tale, they're a cheeky pair.

Unseen Threads

The spider spins a shiny web,
Saying, "Hey, my silk, I'll ebb!"
Catching flies with utmost flair,
As ants march past with a little air.

The wind whispers tales of yore,
Of seeds that traveled to explore.
A sunflower sways, saying, "More!"
As clouds giggle, watching the core.

In soil, a worm throws a rave,
Digging deep and feeling brave.
While moles in hats misbehave,
Dancing with roots, their lives to save.

Invisible threads tie them tight,
In every garden, a playful sight.
With laughter shared in warm daylight,
Nature's jesters, oh what delight!

The Life of Leaves

Leaves whisper secrets in the breeze,
As squirrels scamper with rambunctious ease.
"Hey, let's jump!" says one as it sees,
A branch as a slide, what fun to tease!

In autumn, they fall like confetti bright,
Dancing down in a swirling flight.
The ground laughs, saying, "What a sight!"
While kids jump in piles, sheer delight.

Then winter comes with a frosty bite,
And bare branches scream, "We've lost our might!"
But come spring, oh what a plight,
With new leaves sprouting, nature's rewrite.

Each leaf has a tale, it wants to share,
Of sunny days and storms laid bare.
In their colors, stories flare,
A merry gathering, beyond compare!

Fragrant Fragments

Petals flutter, rotund they giggle,
Beneath the sun, they dance and wiggle.
"I smell awesome!" declares a daffodil,
While roses blush, feeling the thrill.

A mint leaf whispers, "Watch my flair!"
"I'm the gum that you love to share!"
While lavender laughs, with fragrant air,
"With all this fun, life's quite a dare!"

In gardens, herbs engage in fun fights,
Competing aromas set dizzy delight.
Basil rolls over, claiming the heights,
While chives bring humor in green tights.

So here's to blooms, and all things bright,
Each scent a story, a fragrant plight.
Together they sing through day and night,
In this wild garden, pure delight!

Colorful Cadences

In the garden where giggles bloom,
Dancing daisies twirl in the loom.
Sunflowers wear hats, quite absurd,
Listening close, you can hear a word.

Bees don their suits, buzzing in style,
Telling the flowers to smile a while.
Butterflies flutter, a colorful crew,
Whispering secrets they only knew.

Rain drops tap-dance on leaves so green,
A jazzy beat in this leafy scene.
Worms with top hats slide through the dirt,
Throwing a party, not caring if they spurt.

Nature's a clown, always ready to jest,
With each blooming flower, it feels like a fest.
In this folly of flora, laughter resounds,
As every sprout gleefully spins round.

Sowing Seeds of Change

A little seed said, "Oh, what a trip!"
"I'll grow up tall with a funky hip.
I'll sprout my leaves and do a jig,
Shake it all out, I'm feeling big!"

The wind gave a laugh, swirling about,
Turning the garden into a shout.
Raindrops rolled in on a slippery glide,
Complaining, "Why's this life such a ride?"

The carrots were busy planning their dreams,
"Let's become fries and join the streams!"
Potatoes giggled from underground dens,
"Life is a mash-up; we'll be good friends!"

So they plotted and schemed in the sun,
Planting their hopes, oh what fun!
In the patch of laughter, change took hold,
Harvesting giggles worth more than gold.

Rhythms of the Earth

The earth beats a drum, thump-thump-thump,
  As ants form a band with a little grump.
  Dirt and roots, they're shaking in place,
    Creating a rhythm no one can trace.

Flowers sway to the bass of the breeze,
While bushes are buzzed by the giggling trees.
  Caterpillars groove, wearing bright hues,
    Making their own funky dance moves.

The sun cracked a joke, lighting the sky,
While clouds drifted in with a puff and a sigh.
  Grass blades kicked up, do-si-do in pairs,
Bouncing and laughing, tossing their flares.

Every inch of soil knows how to play,
  With each tiny sprout, there's a ballet.
  Nature's a symphony, silly and bright,
Creating a concert from morning till night.

Canvases of the Cosmos

Stars are artists, painting with flair,
Dipping their brushes in dark, chilly air.
Galaxies whirl in a cartoonish dance,
Twinkling away in a sparkly trance.

The moon wears a smile, a cheese-colored grin,
While comets zoom past with a whoosh and a spin.
Asteroids tumble, tripping through space,
Unplanned adventures in a cosmic race.

Each planet is dressed up in wild, wacky threads,
With colors that sparkle and dance to dreads.
Jupiter juggles, and Saturn claps,
While Mars tells tall tales with no time for naps.

In the universe's gallery, laughter erupts,
As meteors fall, so much fun it erupts.
With every big bang, a story's conceived,
In this cosmic canvas, we all believe.

Unfurling Verses of Nature

In the garden, laughter grows,
Bumblebees wear tiny clothes.
Worms debate the best of soil,
While daisies dance and giggle, loyal.

Sunflowers stretch to catch a breeze,
Competing with the buzzing bees.
They twist and turn, their stems are bent,
Who knew plants could be so content?

Raindrops plop like plucky clowns,
Splashing puddles, sporting frowns.
But after storms, the colors pop,
As nature starts its joyful hop.

So come and see this leafy play,
Where laughter grows in bright array.
With roots that stretch and stems that twine,
Nature's script is truly divine!

Blossoms of the Heart

In the garden of love, we sow,
Hearts shaped like buds all aglow.
They bloom and burst with thoughts of cheer,
Sprouting giggles, spreading near.

Dandelions whisper love's decree,
While tulips wink so playfully.
Roses wear their thorns with pride,
In this love, we find our guide.

Sunshine flirts with every breeze,
Tickling leaves like childhood tease.
While petals fall, they slowly waltz,
In this dance, love never faults.

So gather round this vibrant space,
Where joy and fragrance intertwine with grace.
With every bloom, a silly jest,
In our hearts, the sweetest fest!

Growth Between the Lines

Between the lines, where secrets creep,
Worms read poetry while we sleep.
They giggle at our solemn prose,
Turning pages as the garden grows.

We scribble dreams in leafy notes,
Where butterflies wear polka-dots.
And ants parade with tiny flags,
Marching proudly, no time for snags.

The sun becomes a fiery quill,
Writing jokes that make us thrill.
A playful breeze recites a rhyme,
While flowers blush, and bees keep time.

So flip the pages, join the fun,
In the garden, we've just begun.
With laughter sprouting everywhere,
Between each line, the joy we share!

Roots of Resilience

Beneath the soil, the roots conspire,
With wit and charm that won't tire.
They cackle softly, weaving tales,
Of thrifty plants that dance and sail.

Through storms and floods, they never pout,
Instead, they twist and laugh about.
Oh, how they stretch, unwavering might,
Growing strong in laughter, light.

With every struggle, they interlace,
Using humor to embrace.
From cracks in concrete, wildflowers peek,
Sassy and bold, they start to speak.

So raise a glass to roots so grand,
Turning troubles into strands.
In resilience, we've found the key,
To plant our joy, wild and free!

Threads of the Tapestry

In a garden where thoughts dance,
Seeds of laughter take their chance.
Frogs in top hats croak a tune,
While daisies sway and puff balloons.

Rabbits wear their finest coats,
Knitting dreams with tiny coats.
A dandelion whispers bold,
'Grow your dreams, let them unfold!'

Butterflies boast, 'What a sight!
Wings of colors, pure delight.'
Insects join the lively spree,
Planting giggles in the free.

Every root and every sprout,
Tells a story, sparkles out.
In this tapestry of cheer,
Nature croons, 'Stay longer here!'

Sunlit Sonatas

Under sunlight, tunes emerge,
Worms in sync with nature's urge.
A ladybug plays the flute,
While crickets strum their favorite root.

Grass blades sway, a playful game,
Each one strutting, not the same.
Bees dance round, like ballet pros,
Buzzing 'Hey, we're here, do you suppose?'

Clouds join in with cotton cheers,
Dancing lightly through our years.
A flower shouts, 'Encore, encore!'
As petals sway, we beg for more!

Nature's band, oh what a dream,
All together, like a team.
With whispers soft and giggles loud,
Sunlit sonatas draw a crowd!

Harmonies of the Seedling

Beneath the soil, a party brews,
Little roots in joyful hues.
They wiggle and squirm with glee,
Rooting for the big leafy spree!

Tiny sprouts whisper secrets deep,
In their beds, where no one's peeped.
'Look at us, we're growing tall!'
They giggle softly, 'Catch us all!'

Raindrops tap a funny beat,
As petals sway, don't miss a seat!
The sun peeks in, with winks so bright,
'Come out, come out!' they cheer, 'What a sight!'

Nature sings in silly tones,
With each bloom, it playfully moans.
A serenade from every seam,
Harmonies of each living dream!

When Shadows Bud

In twilight's hold, the garden laughs,
Shadows dance like hungry chaffs.
A gnome with shades gives a nod,
To sleepy flowers on their pod.

Beneath the moon, the bugs convene,
Planning pranks in soft green sheen.
'Should we tickle a tulip's toes?
Or splash the pond? Oh, who knows?'

With giggles rising, frogs declare,
'It's shadow play, so do beware!'
As crickets play their nighttime score,
Each bud whispers, 'More, more, more!'

The laughter cools, the daylight sings,
Budding mischief has its wings.
When shadows bud and joy takes flight,
The garden's heart glows through the night!

Scribbles in the Soil

In garden beds where carrots lie,
A squirrel dreams of pie in the sky.
With tiny seeds, he starts to plot,
A salad party—right on the spot!

Sunflowers giggle, waving around,
"Who stole our shade? Not to be found!"
Tomatoes blush beneath their veil,
Whispering secrets, ripe and pale.

Frogs croak out a symphony near,
While butterflies chase their dreams, oh dear!
Mice play tag on the leafy floor,
What fun to be a plant by the door!

And when night falls, stars like eyes,
Peer down at gardens, oh what a guise!
The roots below, they chuckle tight,
"Growing's a joke, but we do it right!"

Growing in Silhouettes

In shadowed corners, plants discuss,
Why lettuce always makes a fuss.
They stretch their leaves, oh what a sight!
Dreaming of salad, dressed just right.

Cacti giggle with spiky grins,
"Who needs water? We're full of wins!"
Succulents chime in, saying with glee,
"Join the dry side, it's the place to be!"

Sunshine drizzles like honey sweet,
While peas and beans take to their feet.
With every leap, they laugh and cheer,
"Growing together is the best of cheer!"

But behind them lurks the frisky weed,
"I'm the life of the party, yes indeed!"
With tangled roots, it dances wild,
A plantish prankster, nature's own child.

Enchanted Ecosystems

In a world where mushrooms wear hats,
Earthworms tell tales of sly little bats.
A ladybug laughs, "I've got the moves,
Watch me groove with the roots as it soothes!"

Frogs in chorus croak out a tune,
To the rhythm of flowers, like a soft noon.
"Hop along, don't be shy or slow,
Join the dance, let your petals glow!"

Each bug a dancer, each leaf a stage,
They twirl and spin, releasing their rage.
"Who says plants can't have a grand show?
We're blooming stars, come watch us grow!"

And if you listen as twilight creeps,
You'll hear them plotting their midnight leaps,
For in this realm of green delight,
Growing's just a reason to dance all night!

Harmonizing Growth

With roots entwined, they sing in tune,
Beneath the smiles of the merry moon.
"Let's throw a party to celebrate air,
Invite the rain, and don't forget flair!"

Beans strum their vines, a jazzy beat,
Pumpkins sway and shuffle their feet.
"Let's toast to growth with a muddy cheer,
For every sprout that dares to appear!"

The breeze whispers secrets, soft and bright,
Caressing leaves under starlit night.
"Not just a garden, we're a fun crew,
Each petal a note, each stem a clue!"

And in this habitat, laughter roams,
Where every seed knows it has a home.
Together they thrive, in harmony's call,
The great garden concert embracing them all!

Songs of Soil and Sky

In the garden, seeds start to dance,
Wiggling to the sun's bright glance.
Earthworms giggle, turn and twirl,
Nature's fun, let laughter unfurl.

A tomato sings, a carrot cheers,
With silly voices, no room for fears.
As daisies shout, 'We're growing tall!',
Bumblebees buzz, having a ball!

Rain drops fall with a splashing tune,
Puddles laugh, reflecting the moon.
Bright green sprouts wear tiny hats,
While snails slide by with acrobatic splats!

So let's all join, in this garden grand,
Dance with the flowers, take a stand.
For life is funny, playfully spry,
In the soil below, and the sky up high!

Waves of Green Awakening

The grass does a jig, all swaying about,
While little ants crawl, shaping their route.
With a whiff of pollen, the daisies laugh,
"Who's the prettiest? It's a flower staff!"

The sun's a jolly fellow, warming the ground,
Making leaves chuckle, not a frown to be found.
A whispering breeze joins the playful spree,
Tickling the stems, wild and free!

Oh, the beans are gossiping, who will climb high?
They hold witty debates, under the blue sky.
Each sprout has a story, to giggle and share,
In this wave of green, joy's everywhere!

As the moon peeks down with a knowing grin,
The vegetables chuckle, let the fun begin.
For every seed planted, comes tales anew,
In the waves of green, where the laughter grew!

Dreams in the Dirt

Down in the dirt, where the gnomes have a ball,
The carrots wear hats, while the radishes brawl.
"Is this really dirt, or a sandy beach?"
Said a tiny potato, "Life's full of preach!"

The flowers spread tales of their day in the sun,
"Oh, how we danced, it was just so much fun!"
With roots all entangled, they joke and they cheer,
While a beet sings a tune, for all buds to hear.

A ladybug strolls with an air of great flair,
"I'll race you to that leaf, if you're willing to dare!"
With worms as the crowd, they gather around,
In this dream of the dirt, pure joy can be found.

At night, under starlight, they twinkle and gleam,
Telling tall tales of each daring dream.
The soil's a theater, with nature's delight,
Where laughter and joy sparkle through the night!

Currents of Growth

Through the cracks in the pavement, the dandelions spread,
Spinning wild stories in a world of their thread.
"Why did the flower cross the road?" they all chirp,
"To get to the sun, without a single burp!"

The roots curl and twist, like they're doing a show,
While fungi above giggle, putting on a glow.
"Let's grow in circles, we can dance with ease!"
Cheered a sprout with a wiggle, swaying in the breeze.

Up above the soil, the sky holds its breath,
While the clouds whisper secrets, as if courting death.
The sun beams a smile, like a jester so bright,
While veggies make up legends, of their wild flight!

With laughter erupting, the garden's a play,
With insects and plants in a comedic fray.
For in each little sprout, a tale's just begun,
In these currents of growth, we all share the fun!

Patterns in the Plume

A feather flew by, thought it could tell,
The secrets of flight, and how to yell.
It flapped like a fish, but couldn't find air,
Bumping into clouds, gave them quite a scare.

The birds laughed aloud, 'What a comical feat!'
A plume on the ground, with no need for a seat.
They chirped and they sang, with joy in their wings,
As the feather sat squashed, dreaming of springs.

It rolled with the breeze, gained friends like a joke,
A worm did a dance, said, "I'm not just smoke!"
Together they tumbled, in nature's small game,
Each giggle and wiggle, a gust of pure fame.

So here's to the plume, that laughs while it flies,
Turning blunders to tales under sunlit skies.
With each twist and turn, they spread with delight,
A merry little journey, from morning to night.

The Language of Leaves

Leaves speak in whispers, a language so sly,
They gossip with branches, in the softest of sighs.
"Did you see that squirrel? He's fashionably late!"
"Or the ants with their hats? Oh, they think they're so great!"

In vibrant green coats, they dance in the air,
A shimmy and shake, with fabulous flair.
"Who needs a breeze when we have the moon?"
"Let's twirl and let's twist, till we fade away soon!"

The flowers all chuckle, "Those leaves are absurd,
They flutter and flutter, haven't you heard?"
Yet together they sway, in a riveting tale,
Of a leafy parade, in a charming detail.

So heed this advice, from the green and the grand,
Take joy in your chatter, and take joy in your stand.
For each laugh is a note in this symphonic play,
And the world's a bright canvas, in its own quirky way.

Petals in the Wind

Petals were planning a grand little spree,
"Let's dance with the wind, and be wild and free!"
But one got too dizzy, and jumped on a bee,
"Oops! My apologies, I'm just trying to be!"

The rose rolled right over, into a bright daisy,
"Chill out, little buddy, you're acting too hazy!"
They spun through the garden, a frolicsome crew,
Stirring up laughter, as they spun and they flew.

A tulip chimed in, "Why don't we all glide?"
With a twirl and a spin, they whirled side by side.
Over grass, round the gate, until they were spent,
Shouting, "What fun! A fine day to be bent!"

So heed this tale of petals so gay,
Find joy in the swerve, and dance in your way.
For each slip and trip, is a giggle divine,
As we flow with the breeze, and let our hearts shine!

Currents of Creation

In the brook, little fish launched a chatty debate,
"Are we swimming upstream, or just staying out late?"
With bubbles and splashes, the talk became wild,
As minnows made puns, and gilled with a smile.

"Let's create a ripple, and giggle with glee!"
Said the water to rocks, "Come dance with me!"
So they twisted and tumbled, like leaves in a race,
All grinning and laughing, in this watery place.

The wind joined the fun with a whoosh and a roar,
Spinning tales of old, while the waves hit the shore.
"Who knew creation could giggle so much?"
As the current's cool flow gave the universe such.

In this mingled creation, there's humor afloat,
The world's like a laugh, in a well-timed quote.
So dive in and play, let the waters surprise,
As we drift on the currents, beneath the wide skies.

Verses of Verdancy

In the garden, seeds do giggle,
Wiggling worms with a little wiggle.
Chasing rain with playful cheer,
Watering cans hold their beer.

In dawn's light, morning glories dance,
Bees in tuxedos doing their prance.
Flowers wear hats, oh what a sight,
Sunflowers salute, feeling just right.

Tomato plants hold a cookout feast,
Courgettes gossip like a bunch of beasts.
Radishes tease with a red, round face,
While carrots hide in their leafy place.

With every sprout, they all do cheer,
Roots intertwining in good, joyful cheer.
Nature's clowns, in soil they play,
The garden's giggles light up the day.

The Melodic Meadow

In the meadow, crickets recite,
Singing loudly into the night.
Butterflies dance with vibrant flair,
Winks at daisies, a flirty affair.

Grasshoppers hop like they own the scene,
Plotting pranks on the flowers' sheen.
They flick their toes, creating a beat,
While daisies tap with pedal-like feet.

The sun in its glory, a radiant tease,
Inviting all critters to join the breeze.
Ladybugs laugh as they take a spin,
Promising more fun, let the games begin!

In this whimsical stretch of green,
Life's simple joys are high on the scene.
For in nature's tune, laughter aligns,
As laughter frolics and sunlight shines.

Cycle of the Seasons

Springtime brings its flashy attire,
Bunnies leaping on a high wire.
Flowers bloom, wearing hats so bright,
Join the jester-birds in their flight.

Summer sizzles like a hot pan,
Ice cream cones in every hand.
Squirrels plotting snacks so divine,
Chasing shadows, oh how they shine!

Autumn leaves fall, a crispy parade,
Pumpkin spice in every shade.
The squirrels stash nuts with clumsy glee,
While the grand trees weave their symphony.

Winter arrives, dressed in a coat,
Snowmen laugh, twirling in a boat.
With hot cocoa cheers, we toast the cold,
As seasons turn, stories unfold.

Tides of Transformation

The ocean whispers tales so grand,
As waves frolic and dance on sand.
Seagulls cackle, soaring high,
Playing tag with the cottony sky.

With each tide, secrets unfold,
Shells tell stories that time's retold.
Starfish lounge like it's their spa,
While crabs perform a clumsy cha-cha.

When the moon rises, it casts a spell,
Bubbles giggle, they rise and swell.
With squishy jelly, the sea laughs loud,
As kelp dances in a flowing crowd.

And in this spectacle of sea's domain,
Life's joyous heartbeat remains the same.
From the deep blue grandeurs to shores so fine,
The tides of change keep time with rhyme.

Boughs and Ballads

In the orchard, trees dance tall,
Singing songs, it's quite a ball!
Branches sway with laugh and cheer,
While squirrels strut, no hint of fear.

Leaves jiggle to the breezy tune,
Bumblebees buzz, a buzzing boon!
Carrots crack jokes beneath the ground,
In a patch where humor's found.

Funky fungi play hide and seek,
Making faces, oh so cheek!
Roots below do rhythmic flips,
Nature's giggles, in sways and slips.

In this garden, joy's the seed,
Like laughter sprouting, take the lead!
With every bloom, a chuckle shared,
In harmony, we're unprepared.

The Art of Growth

Watch the sprout, it wobbles proud,
Giggling grains beneath a cloud.
Photosynthesis, quite the show,
Leaves wearing sunglasses, green glow!

Caterpillars munch and munch,
Never stop, always on lunch!
Buds pop up with puns galore,
Knock-knock jokes till they can't snore.

Roots do yoga in the earth,
Stretching wide for what it's worth.
They whisper secrets to the stones,
About life's jokes and silly tones.

Flowers bloom in carnival hues,
With petals like balloons, oh please!
Laughing bees in merry flight,
Dance in circles, pure delight.

Whispers of Wildness

Among the wild, where critters play,
A hedgehog tells jokes every day.
Twigs are giggling underfoot,
While worms wear hats, oh what a hoot!

Tall grasses sway in cheeky grace,
Tickling noses, a merry chase.
The wind, a jester, twists and twirls,
Teasing daisies with gentle swirls.

Frogs croak rhymes by moonlight's beam,
With fireflies joining in the theme.
Mice and owls, they laugh at night,
In this wild theater, pure delight.

Nature's jesters, a carefree bunch,
Spreading smiles in every hunch.
With every rustle, a giggle found,
Wildness whispers, joy abound.

Melodies of Metamorphosis

From egg to bug, such a surprise,
Each tiny critter has big dreams to rise.
Turning flips, it's quite the feat,
In a world where green is sweet!

Butterflies flapping, wearing bling,
Making transformations a funny fling.
With each flutter, they share a jest,
In colorful garb, they are the best!

Chrysalis cocoons snug on a branch,
Making friends at the metamorph dance.
With laughter in waves and a wink from the moth,
Who knew change could come with such froth?

Every change there's a giggle and glee,
In the best of times, wild and free.
With nature's tunes and goofy plots,
Metamorphosis connects the dots.

Embrace of the Earth

In the soil, we plant our seeds,
Hoping they sprout into our needs.
Worms wiggle with delight and cheer,
Making the garden a comedy sphere.

The daisies dance, they bow and sway,
Critiques from the weeds? They'll rue the day!
With every bloom, there's laughter and glee,
Nature's joke—who knew it could be free?

Echoing with New Beginnings

A sprout peeks out, oh what a sight,
It trips on roots, then takes a flight.
Sunshine giggles, clouds share a grin,
"Who knew that gardening's a win-win?"

A blossom shouts, "I'm the brightest here!"
While mushrooms chuckle, "Have a beer!"
With every bud, the laughter swells,
In this wild circus, nature compels.

Symphony of Sprouts

The sprouts gear up for a wild reprise,
With tiny strings and leafy ties.
A weed says, "Wait, I'm part of the show!"
While daisies argue, "Oh no, no, no!"

Hummingbirds join, with wings that whirl,
They crash the stage in a colorful twirl.
Nature's band plays a tune so wacky,
Even the cacti find it a bit tacky!

Canvas of Colors

A palette spills forth from the ground,
With reds, blues, and yellows around.
Petunias slap paint on a tulip's face,
While violets claim they lead the race.

In this gallery of plants, such delight,
The sun sets low, painting the night.
Laughter and petals, a joyous display,
In nature's masterpiece, we dance and play!

Dance of the Dandelions

In the breeze they twirl and spin,
Little yellow suns wear a grin.
Fluffy heads, they take a leap,
From lawns to skies, in dreams they creep.

With a puff, they spread goodwill,
Childish laughter amplifies the thrill.
They don't worry 'bout where they land,
Just blowing kisses, oh so grand!

A dandelion's bold parade,
On sidewalks and in glades they wade.
While homeowners pull with all their might,
These sprightly blooms just laugh in delight!

So dance away, you little seeds,
On nature's stage, you're all it's needs.
A golden crown on summer's face,
You spread your joy through open space.

Chambers of the Cell

Inside a tiny world, it's true,
Cells are bustling, who knew?
Making copies, doubling fun,
In microscopes, they shine like the sun.

Mitochondria, the power brigade,
Fueling dreams in a playful trade.
With more energy than a dance at night,
They keep the cells feeling just right.

Nucleus shouts, "Don't forget my role!"
With DNA, it's the main goal.
"Let's duplicate, replicate!" they sing,
Creating life, oh what a fling!

So raise a toast to the little guys,
In their chambers, watch them rise.
A dance of life, so small and sweet,
In every heartbeat, they skip a beat!

Harmonies of Life and Light

In forests deep, the sunbeams play,
Creating melodies throughout the day.
Leaves whisper secrets with rustling cheer,
Joining the dance, as the twilight draws near.

Birds chirp a tune, light as a feather,
Compose a symphony, all come together.
With every flutter and every flight,
Nature croons in sheer delight.

From blossoms bright to rivers so clear,
The joyful harmony draws us near.
With laughter linked to every sight,
Life blooms like colors shining bright.

So laugh with flowers and sway with trees,
Join the concert, feel the breeze.
A world where joy invites the night,
In harmonies of life and light!

Pathways of Potential

In every seed, a story waits,
Dreams of trees and garden gates.
With sprouted hope, they aim for the sky,
Unfurling their magic, oh my!

Wiggly worms dig tunnels new,
While roots stretch wide, like spaghetti too.
Adventures await in each leafy nook,
Pathways of potential in every book.

Chasing sunbeams, through fields they roam,
Little sprouts on their way back home.
With silly twists, they wiggle and dance,
Planting promises, giving life a chance.

So let's explore these paths so grand,
Where every foot can make its stand.
In gardens wild, and backyards free,
Potential blooms eternally!

Whispers of Seedlings

In a tiny pot, a seedling sighed,
"Water me, please, I'm somewhat dried!"
With a little dance, it spun around,
"I dream of fruits, not just the ground!"

A worm crawled by with a humorous grin,
"You think you're a star? Just wait 'til you win!"
The seedling chuckled, "Oh, I'll be great!"
"With sun on my leaves, I'll dance on my plate!"

Echoes in the Wind

A dandelion puff, bold and spry,
"I'm off to the heavens, just watch me fly!"
The breeze picked it up, with a twirl and a spin,
"I may come back as a fluff or a pin!"

The trees laughed loud, with branches that sway,
"Catch us if you can, we'll dance all day!"
And through the giggles, the wind did reply,
"I'll scatter your dreams to the faraway sky!"

Roots Beneath the Surface

Roots tangled up like a jumbled yarn,
"Who needs a sweater? We hold up the farm!"
One whispered softly, "Let's wiggle and play,"
"And trip the tomatoes on harvest day!"

Under the soil, they had quite the feud,
"You're too slow! No way you'll get food!"
But as they bickered, a wise potato said,
"Let's work together, we're not all misled!"

Gardens of Tomorrow

In a garden patch, where daisies boast,
"I'm the prettiest flower, I'll make a fine toast!"
A beetroot blushed, "But I'm tasty and sweet,"
"With salads and dips, I'm the real treat!"

Around the corner, the carrots all laughed,
"We're the crunchiest ones, you'll see our craft!"
"Don't be so vain, let's have some fun,
We'll feast on our harvest, all everyone!"

www.ingramcontent.com/pod-product-compliance
Lightning Source LLC
Chambersburg PA
CBHW070315120526
44590CB00017B/2687